Mail Carriers

By JoAnn Early Macken

Reading consultant: Susan Nations, M.Ed., author/literacy coach/consultant

Gareth Stevens Publishing

Please visit our Web site www.garethstevens.com. For a free color catalog of all our high-quality books, call toll free 1-800-542-2595 or fax 1-877-542-2596.

Library of Congress Cataloging-in-Publication Data

Macken, JoAnn Early, 1953-
    Mail carrier / by JoAnn Early Macken.
        p. cm. — (People in my community)
    Summary: Photographs and simple text describe the work done by mail carriers.
    Includes bibliographical references and index.
    ISBN: 978-1-4339-3345-5 (pbk.)
    ISBN: 978-1-4339-3346-2 (6-pack)
    ISBN: 978-1-4339-3344-8 (library binding)
    1. Letter carriers—United States—Juvenile literature.   [1. Letter carriers.   2. Occupations.]
    I. Title. II. Series.
    HE6499.M13   2003
    383'.145'02373—dc21   2002032961

New edition published 2010 by
Gareth Stevens Publishing
111 East 14th Street, Suite 349
New York, NY 10003

New text and images this edition copyright © 2010 Gareth Stevens Publishing

Original edition published 2003 by Weekly Reader® Books
An imprint of Gareth Stevens Publishing
Original edition text and images copyright © 2003 Gareth Stevens Publishing

Art direction: Haley Harasymiw, Tammy Gruenewald
Page layout: Michael Flynn, Katherine A. Goedheer
Editorial direction: Kerri O'Donnell, Diane Laska Swanke

Cover, back cover, p. 1 © Jeff Dunn/Photolibrary/Getty Images; p. 5 © Kim Steele/Photodisc/ Getty Images; pp. 7, 9, 11, 13, 15, 17, 21 by Gregg Andersen; p. 19 © Tim Boyle/Getty Images.

Printed in the United States of America

CPSIA compliance information: Batch #WW10GS: For further information contact Gareth Stevens, New York, New York at 1-800-542-2595.

Table of Contents

Boldface words appear in the glossary.

Here Comes the Mail!

A mail carrier delivers the mail.

First, mail carriers **sort** the mail at the post office.

Each letter and **package** must go to the right **address**. Mail can be delivered only if it has a **stamp**.

address

Some mail carriers walk to deliver the mail. They might carry the mail in a pouch.

pouch

Some mail carriers drive cars or trucks to deliver the mail. They drive from house to house.

truck

2208844

Some mail carriers have the same **route** each day. They deliver mail to homes, businesses, and schools.

Special Clothes

Mail carriers wear special **uniforms**. In the summer, they may wear shorts.

uniform

UNITED STATES
POSTAL SERVICE

In the winter, they wear warmer clothes. Mail carriers work in all kinds of weather.

Mail for Me!

It's fun to get something in the mail!

Glossary

address: the place where mail gets delivered

package: a box or carton with things packed in it

route: a path taken from place to place

sort: to put in order

stamp: something put on mail to show that you paid to send it

uniform: clothing worn by members of a group such as police officers, firefighters, or mail carriers

For More Information

Books

Brown, Risa. *Mail Carriers.*
  Bethany, MO: Fitzgerald Books, 2007.
Marsico, Katie. *Working at the Post Office.*
  Ann Arbor, MI: Cherry Lake Publishing, 2009.
Owen, Ann. *Delivering Your Mail: A Book About Mail Carriers.*
  Mankato, MN: Picture Window Books, 2003.
Thomas, Mary Ann. *A Trip to the Post Office.*
  New York: Rosen Publishing, 2008.
Trumbaur, Lisa. *What Does A Mail Carrier Do?*
  Berkeley Heights, NJ: Enslow Elementary, 2005.

Web Sites
People, Occupations, and Community
http://www.enchantedlearning.com/themes/
communityhelpers.shtml

Publisher's note to educators and parents: Our editors have carefully reviewed these Web sites to ensure that they are suitable for students. Many Web sites change frequently, however, and we cannot guarantee that a site's future contents will continue to meet our high standards of quality and educational value. Be advised that students should be closely supervised whenever they access the Internet.

Index

About the Author

JoAnn Early Macken is the author of children's poetry, two rhyming picture books, *Cats on Judy* and *Sing-Along Song,* and various other nonfiction series. She teaches children to write poetry and received the Barbara Juster Esbensen 2000 Poetry Teaching Award. JoAnn is a graduate of the MFA in Writing for Children Program at Vermont College. She lives in Wisconsin with her husband and their two sons.